Soldiers of the Spanish-American War

Diane Smolinski

Series Consultant:
Lieutenant Colonel G.A. LoFaro

Heinemann Library
Chicago, Illinois

© 2003 Reed Educational & Professional Publishing
Published by Heinemann Library,
an imprint of Reed Educational & Professional
Publishing, Chicago, Illinois

Customer Service 888-454-2279

Visit our website at www.heinemannlibrary.com

Designed by Herman Adler Design
Photo research by Julie Laffin
Printed and bound in the United States by Lake Book
Manufacturing, Inc.

07 06 05 04 03
10 9 8 7 6 5 4 3 2 1

Library of Congress Cataloging-in-Publication Data
Smolinski, Diane, 1950-
  Soldiers of the Spanish-American War / Diane
Smolinski.
      v. cm. -- (Americans at war. The Spanish-American
War)
Includes bibliographical references and index.
Contents: Preparing for war -- Infantry units -- Artillery
units --Cavalry units -- The Rough Riders -- General
William Rufus Shafter --Theodore Roosevelt -- National
guard -- Women in the war -- African and
Native Americans -- The U.S. Navy -- Commodore
George Dewey -- Admiral William Thomas Sampson --
Spanish Army -- Spanish Navy -- Admiral Patricio
Montojo y Pasaron -- Admiral Pascual Cervera y Topete.
   ISBN 1-4034-0173-X
   1. United States. Army--History--Spanish-American
War, 1898--Juvenile literature. 2. United States. Navy--
History--Spanish-American War, 1898--Juvenile
literature. 3. Soldiers--United States--History--19th
century--Juvenile literature. 4. Spanish-American War,
1898--Campaigns--Juvenile literature. [1. Spanish-
American War, 1898. 2. United States. Army--History--
Spanish-American War, 1898. 3. United States. Navy--
History--Spanish-American War, 1898.] I. Title.
   E725 .S66 2002
   973.8'95--dc21
                        2002005086

Acknowledgments
The author and publishers are grateful to the following
for permission to reproduce copyright material:
Contents page, p.14B Peter Newark's Military Pictures;
pp. 4, 12, 15, 18, 21L, 26, 27 The Granger Collection,
New York; pp. 5T, 5B, 7T, 17, 20, 21R, 23, 28
Bettmann/Corbis; pp. 6, 8, 10, 11, 13, 16, 22, 29 Brown
Brothers; pp. 7B, 14T, 24, 25T North Wind Picture
Archives; pp. 19, 25B Library of Congress.

Cover photographs: (main) Brown Brothers, (border,
T-B) Philip James Corwin/Corbis, Reuters NewMedia
Inc./Corbis.

Every effort has been made to contact copyright holders
of any material reproduced in this book. Any omissions
will be rectified in subsequent printings if notice is given
to the publisher.

About the Author
Diane Smolinski is the author of two previous series of
books on the Revolutionary and Civil Wars. She earned
degrees in education from Duquesne and Slippery Rock
Universities and taught in public schools for 28 years.
Diane now writes for teachers, helping them to use
nonfiction books in their classrooms. She currently
lives in Florida with her husband, Henry, and their
cat, Pepper.

Special thanks to Lt. Colonel Guy LoFaro for his
interest and expertise in military history. May all
young readers be inspired by his passion for history
to extend their learning well beyond the words written
on these pages.

About the Consultant
G.A. LoFaro is a lieutenant colonel in the U.S. Army
currently stationed at Fort McPherson, Georgia. After
graduating from West Point, he was commissioned in
the infantry. He has served in a variety of positions in
the 82nd Airborne Division, the Ranger Training
Brigade, and Second Infantry Division in Korea. He
has a Masters Degree in U.S. History from the
University of Michigan and is completing his Ph.D in
U.S. History at the State University of New York at
Stony Brook. He has also served six years on the West
Point faculty where he taught military history to cadets.

On the cover: This picture shows American soldiers at camp during the Spanish-American War.
On the contents page: Theodore Roosevelt (on horseback) leads his Rough Riders up Kettle Hill in Santiago, Cuba, on July 1, 1898.

Some words are shown in bold, **like this.**
You can find out what they mean by looking in the glossary.

Contents

Introduction

When the United States could not convince Spain to give up control of Cuba, the two nations went to war. The U.S. declared war on Spain on April 25, 1898.

The Spanish-American War was fought in two different parts of the world. Battles occurred on two **fronts:** in the Caribbean Sea and in the Pacific Ocean. Even though the war officially lasted only about four months, it ended centuries of Spanish control over the islands of Cuba, Puerto Rico, and the Philippines.

United States and Spanish armies and navies as well as local **resistance fighters** in Cuba, Puerto Rico, and the Philippines were involved in the fighting. The spirit and courage of all men involved in the fighting was important in determining the outcome of this "splendid little war."

*Spain was so far away from its **colonies** of Cuba, Puerto Rico, and the Philippines, that it was often difficult to protect them.*

1898 Gazette

"A Splendid Little War"

John Hay, U.S. Secretary of State in 1898, called the Spanish-American War "a splendid little war" because it lasted only four months and few soldiers were killed in the fighting.

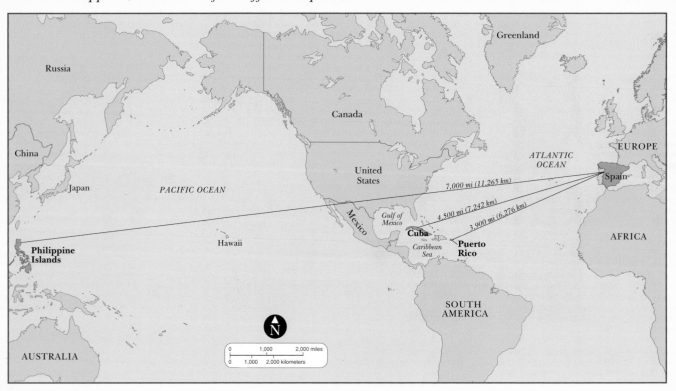

Preparing for War

After the **Civil War** (1861–1865), the United States no longer kept a large army. Individual states continued to maintain their own units, called the **National Guard.** By the time the Spanish-American War began, the United States **Regular Army** had less than 30,000 men assigned to posts scattered throughout the country. These men spent many years after the Civil War fighting against North American Indians on **frontier** lands.

When war was declared in 1898, **Congress** had to act quickly to prepare the nation. Congress voted to double the size of the regular army and to increase the number of volunteer soldiers that each state could send to fight. They passed laws allowing the government to spend money for ships, supplies, and soldiers.

*More than 10,000 officers and 200,000 **enlisted** men served in the U.S. Army during the Spanish-American War.*

In order to encourage men to volunteer for military service, the U.S. government increased the pay for soldiers. They sometimes offered bonuses to those who joined as well.

1898 Gazette

Tampa, Florida was the embarkation headquarters for the U.S. Army during the Spanish-American War.

- Tampa to Havana, Cuba—335 miles (539 kilometers)

- Tampa to San Juan, Puerto Rico—1,235 miles (1,988 kilometers)

- Tampa to Manila, Philippines—9,111 miles (14,663 kilometers)

No Well-Designed Plan

Even though many men volunteered for military duty, the United States government did not have a well-designed plan to fight the Spanish. They knew little about the strength and ability of the Spanish **forces** that they would be fighting against. Few reliable maps of Cuba, Puerto Rico, and the Philippines were available at this time.

State of the Army in 1898

The United States Army lacked trained soldiers, supplies, and modern weapons. The Army and Navy would have to work together to **transport** the army and its equipment across oceans to distant islands where the war would be fought. Fighting a war away from American soil would present many new challenges.

Men and supplies were loaded onto ships in ports in the southeastern United States. These soldiers were on their way to Cuba.

*These marines fought with Commodore Dewey and the Pacific **Fleet.***

The U.S. **Regular Army,** the **National Guard,** and volunteer units consisted of **infantry, cavalry,** and **artillery** soldiers. All were anxious to join the war in Cuba after the sinking of the USS *Maine* in Havana Harbor.

Nearly 280,000 sailors, marines, and soldiers volunteered to serve in the Spanish-American War. Because this war lasted only four months, it ended before many of these soldiers could be trained and sent to the different war **fronts.** During the war, 5,462 men died; only a little over 300 men died from battle wounds. Most men died from diseases such as malaria and yellow fever.

1898 Gazette

- Malaria is a disease carried by certain mosquitoes that cause a person to have severe chills and a high fever.

- Yellow fever is a tropical disease carried by mosquitoes that causes a high fever and a yellowing of the skin.

- Even though nearly 280,000 men served in the Spanish-American War, this was not a great number compared to the more than three million men who had fought in the **Civil War** from 1861 to 1865.

These sailors are standing next to one of the USS Maine's *torpedo tubes. The* Maine *exploded and sank in Havana Harbor on February 15, 1898. Many Americans blamed Spain for the explosion. Today, people still do not agree on what really happened to the* Maine.

Infantry Units

Most soldiers in the United States Army were part of the infantry. When the infantry needed to travel to the islands of Cuba, Puerto Rico, and the Philippines, they went by boat. Infantrymen generally traveled from battle to battle on foot.

Infantrymen had to carry their equipment. Some of the equipment issued to a **regular army** infantry soldier during this time was:

- a rifle—the basic weapon of the infantry;
- a bayonet—a long knife that attached to the end of the rifle for hand-to-hand combat;
- a cartridge belt—a belt that held up to 100 bullets for the rifle;
- mess equipment—a spoon, a steel knife, a fork, a tin cup, and a container that was used as a dish;
- a poncho—a pullover raincoat;
- a tent—for shelter; and
- different types of uniforms.

*Once the war began, infantry units were issued **khaki**-colored pants. Many continued to wear the dark blue colors of an earlier issue. Some also wore a light tan or gray **slouch hat**.*

Many of the infantry units trained in New Orleans, Louisiana; Tampa, Florida; and Mobile, Alabama. By training in the southern heat, soldiers would become used to the tropical climate of the islands where war was being fought. These cities were also ocean ports. Soldiers would be close to the ships that would **transport** them to these distant islands.

We know these volunteer troops in Los Angeles were infantry soldiers because of the two crossed rifles on their hats. A number above the cross indicated the **regiment,** *while a letter below the cross indicated a specific company in the regiment.*

1898 Gazette

To **enlist** in the U.S. Army in 1898, men had to:

- be between the ages of 18 and 35;

- have good character;

- have no diseases;

- be able to speak English;

- be a citizen of the U.S. or intend to become a citizen;

- get special permission from the commander of the unit if they were married;

- take a physical;

- complete enlistment papers; and

- take an **oath.**

Artillery Units

Some soldiers who joined the army were trained to fire and maintain cannons called artillery. The men, the cannons, the equipment, and the horses needed to transport the equipment were called a battery.

A cannon could be attached to a two-wheeled frame so it could be easily moved. Army pack mules were used to pull wagons and transport some of the equipment. Roads were poor on most of these islands, making it difficult for artillery units to move equipment to the battle sites.

Artillery moved with the **infantry** into battle. It shelled the enemy that was hiding in **trenches** or behind **fortifications.**

Artillerymen had to care for the horses or mules that pulled the artillery pieces, as well as care for the cannons and other equipment.

1898 Gazette

- Today, the army mule is the mascot of the United States Military Academy at West Point.

- **Regular Army** artillerymen dressed much the same as infantrymen, in **khaki**-colored pants and blue shirts. A difference appeared in the color of the stripe on the pants. Artillerymen wore a red stripe, while infantrymen wore white. **Slouch hats** were also often worn. In 1898, uniforms were in short supply; so volunteers' uniforms varied from the standard issue.

Cavalry Units

The cavalry were U.S. Army soldiers who were trained to ride horses in battle. Cavalry units were also used to scout ahead of the infantry and artillery. They gathered information about the opposing army's location and number of soldiers.

Some equipment used by a cavalry trooper included:

- a carbine—a type of rifle, much shorter in length than the one carried by infantrymen;
- a saber—a curved sword;
- a pistol—a handgun; and
- a horse.

During the Spanish-American War, many cavalry soldiers fought in battle without horses. Sometimes a lack of space on the ships transporting troops and equipment caused the horses to be left behind. Also, many horses drowned before they were able to swim to shore from the transport ships. When cavalrymen fought in battle without their horses, they were called dismounted cavalry.

Most cavalrymen wore the newer khaki-colored pants, but many continued to wear the dark blue colors of an earlier issue. Like the infantrymen, they wore slouch hats.

11

The Rough Riders

One of the most recognized U.S. Army units that fought in Cuba during the Spanish-American War was the 1st U.S. Volunteer Cavalry, also known as the "Rough Riders."

Although many of the men came from the southwestern part of the United States, men from all parts of the country joined this cavalry **regiment.** The Rough Riders trained in San Antonio, Texas. Then they traveled to Tampa, Florida, to board ships for Cuba.

The first commander of the Rough Riders was Colonel Leonard Wood. He was a medical doctor respected for fighting battles against the Indians in the **frontier** lands. Lieutenant Colonel Theodore Roosevelt soon became the commander after Wood was promoted. He led the famous attack on Kettle Hill on July 1, 1898, that was part of the Battle of San Juan Heights in Cuba. The Rough Riders charged the Spanish positions, driving them from Kettle Hill.

Roosevelt's charge on Kettle Hill eventually led to the capture of the city of Santiago, Cuba and the end of the war. This painting inaccurately shows the Rough Riders on horseback. Roosevelt was the only one to have a horse during this battle.

1898 Gazette

San Juan Heights

- The San Juan Heights were a group of hills surrounding the city of Santiago, Cuba. The Spanish chose this high ground as the site from which to defend the city.

- Even though the Rough Riders were a cavalry unit, most of their horses did not make it to the Battle of San Juan Heights. So, the Rough Riders had to attack on foot. Their commander, Lieutenant Colonel Theodore Roosevelt, did ride a horse.

- Theodore Roosevelt's horse was named Little Texas.

General William Rufus Shafter (1835–1906)

Before the War

William Rufus Shafter was born in what is now Michigan on October 16, 1835. He became a schoolteacher, but when the **Civil War** began in 1861 he volunteered to join the army and was made an officer. After the Civil War ended, Shafter decided to make the army his career.

During the War

In 1898, William Shafter was made the commander of the U.S. Army in Cuba. His troops marched to capture the city of Santiago, but Shafter became ill and could not lead his troops in this important battle.

After the War

Shafter served in the army until his retirement in 1901. He died in California in 1906.

William Shafter, Commander of the 5th Army Corps, was 62 years old when the Spanish-American War began. He is shown here (center) riding through the city of Santiago after the Battle of San Juan Heights.

Theodore Roosevelt (1858–1919)

Before the War

Theodore Roosevelt was born in New York City on October 27, 1858 to a wealthy family. He attended Harvard College in Massachusetts and was interested in studying and then working in **politics.** In 1897, Roosevelt gained an important position in politics when he was appointed the assistant secretary of the U.S. Navy.

During the War

Wanting to take part in the Spanish-American War, Theodore (Teddy) Roosevelt **resigned** as the assistant secretary of the Navy and joined the 1st U.S. Volunteer **Cavalry,** also known as the "Rough Riders." Newspaper reports of his successful charge on Kettle Hill in Cuba made him famous.

Theodore Roosevelt as assistant secretary of the U.S. Navy (top), and during the Spanish-American War (bottom).

1898 Gazette

- Theodore Roosevelt was awarded the **Medal of Honor** for his part in the fighting on Kettle Hill. His son, Theodore Roosevelt, Jr., also won the Medal of Honor for his part in the fighting on Utah Beach during the D-day invasion in 1944 during World War II.

- Before being appointed the Lieutenant Colonel of the Rough Riders, Teddy Roosevelt held several other jobs. Some of his jobs were:

  - New York State Assemblyman from New York City;
  - Police Commissioner of New York City; and
  - Ranch owner in the Dakota territory.

After the War

Theodore Roosevelt continued his career in politics after the Spanish-American War. In 1898, he was elected the governor of the state of New York. In 1900, William McKinley ran for president of the United States, and Theodore Roosevelt was his **running mate.** They won the election, making Roosevelt the vice president of the United States. On September 14, 1901, President McKinley was **assassinated,** and Roosevelt became the 26th president of the United States.

While Roosevelt was president, the United States became more involved in world politics. In the U.S., he was concerned about the environment and laws that brought fair treatment for workers and industries. He was reelected in 1904, but chose not to run again in 1908. He died on January 6, 1919.

*Roosevelt believed it was important to build a strong military **force** to protect the United States, but he avoided using physical force to carry out his policies. As president, he used the saying, "Speak softly and carry a big stick," to explain this idea.*

1898 Gazette

- The Teddy Bear was named after him.
- During the time Theodore Roosevelt was president:
  - the Wright brothers successfully flew the first airplane;
  - the construction of the Panama Canal began; and
  - the Model T Ford was built.

The National Guard

During wartime, it was necessary to increase the size of the army. The government encouraged men to volunteer in the individual state military units called the National Guard.

Although many men volunteered, there was not enough money to properly equip such great numbers. Most soldiers were using old weapons. Many units were from northern states that had wool uniforms for the colder weather. These men would need proper clothing for the tropical climate in which they would be training and fighting. Since the government did not have much money to spend at this time, many of the volunteers needed to use at least part of their state's National Guard uniforms, rather than receiving a standard U.S. Army uniform.

Officers now faced the difficult task of training and organizing the individual National Guard units into an effective army.

National Guard units added nearly 100,000 men to the ranks of the U.S. military. Below, the 9th New York National Guard leaves New York City for camp.

Women in the War

In 1898, women were not allowed to **enlist** in the military. However, nurses were hired by the U.S. government to help care for soldiers involved in the Spanish-American War. Even though some men in the U.S. Army were trained as medical workers, disease and unsanitary conditions raised a need for more help.

More than 1,000 women signed contracts to provide nursing care for the army at this time, each earning $30 a month. Although women nurses were not paid equally or given any military rank, they played an important part for the U.S. military during the Spanish-American War.

These nurses were hired to work on the hospital ship, Relief, *that sailed in the waters around the island of Cuba during the Spanish-American War. Not long after the war in 1901, an official Army Nurse Corps was established.*

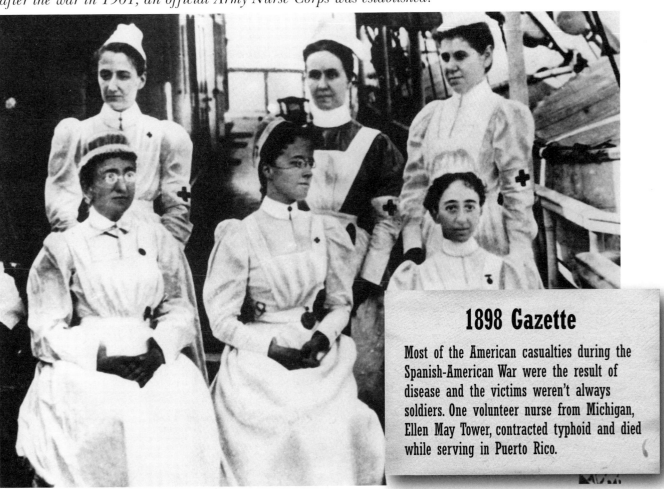

1898 Gazette

Most of the American casualties during the Spanish-American War were the result of disease and the victims weren't always soldiers. One volunteer nurse from Michigan, Ellen May Tower, contracted typhoid and died while serving in Puerto Rico.

African and Native Americans

Before the War

In 1866, **Congress** allowed six **segregated regiments** of African-American soldiers to be formed—two **cavalry** and four **infantry** units. Many young African-American men decided to join the army, as it offered them a steady job. Many white citizens did not want African-American troops in their communities, so the U.S. Army sent these troops out to the western **frontier** to control the Indian population.

During the War: In the U.S. Army

African-American soldiers served in U.S. Army Volunteer (Colored) Infantry and Cavalry units. Five soldiers from these units were awarded the **Medal of Honor.** The U.S. Army's 9th and 10th Cavalry units fought beside the Rough Riders at the battles on the San Juan Heights in Cuba.

Members of the U.S. 10th (Colored) Cavalry pose for a picture following the capture of San Juan Hill in Cuba.

1898 Gazette

- The original six regiments of African-American soldiers were called the 9th and 10th Cavalry and the 38th, 39th, 40th, and 41st Infantry Regiments. In 1869, the four infantry units were reduced to two. Therefore, at the beginning of the Spanish-American War, there were only four African-American units—the 9th and 10th Cavalry and the 24th and 25th Infantry.

- Cheyenne Indians gave the regiments of African-American soldiers the nickname "Buffalo Soldiers" because of their fighting spirit, like the Indians' sacred buffalo.

Fireman William Lambert (top right), an African American, was a crewmember of the USS Maine *and a member of the ship's baseball team.*

During the War: In the U.S. Navy

African Americans served alongside sailors of all nationalities on navy ships. According to a list of "colored men on board the USS *Maine*, February 15, 1898," 22 of the 30 African Americans aboard the *Maine* died when it exploded. Two African-American sailors received the Medal of Honor, one at the Battle of Santiago and the other a few months before.

Native Americans

Some Native Americans fought in the Spanish-American War as part of the U.S. Volunteers. They were part of the 1st Volunteer Cavalry, or Rough Riders, unit and the 1st Territorial Volunteer Infantry.

1898 Gazette

At this time, African Americans served in the U.S. Navy and U.S. Army but not in the U.S. Marine Corps. The U.S. Marine Corps did not accept African Americans until World War II.

The U.S. Navy

The U.S. Navy was better prepared for war than was the U.S. Army. To protect both shores of the United States, navy ships were positioned along the Atlantic and Pacific coastlines. Compared to the Spanish Navy, the U.S. Navy had more modern and powerful ships.

In the Atlantic

The main U.S. **fleet** was based at Key West, Florida, in the Caribbean Sea. This fleet would support troops in Cuba and Puerto Rico.

In the Pacific

When war was declared, the Pacific Fleet was in China. They quickly set sail for the Philippine Islands. They defeated the Spanish fleet at the Battle of Manila Bay on May 1, 1898.

Throughout the war, navy ships **transported** army troops to the islands of Cuba, Puerto Rico, and the Philippines. These same ships fired their cannons to protect soldiers going ashore. By positioning ships just offshore, it kept the Spanish from resupplying their armies on the islands.

When the Pacific Fleet left China and set sail for the Philippines, ships were painted gray to make them less noticeable to the enemy and all wooden items were thrown overboard.

Commodore George Dewey (1837–1917)

Before the War

George Dewey was born in Vermont on December 26, 1837. He attended college at the **U.S. Naval Academy** and served in the U.S. Navy during the **Civil War.** In 1897, Dewey was appointed the commander of the **Asiatic Squadron** in the Pacific.

During the War

George Dewey is probably most remembered for defeating the Spanish at the Battle of Manila Bay in the Philippines on May 1, 1898. After this battle, Dewey was promoted to admiral by **Congress** and was recognized as a hero.

After the War

Dewey wrote about his victory at Manila Bay and published his autobiography in 1913. He served in the U.S. Navy until his death at age 79.

*In 1857, George Dewey was one of only fifteen **cadets** to graduate from the U.S. Naval Academy. Even though he was bothered by health problems early in his life, he went on to have a long and successful naval career.*

1898 Gazette

Battle of Manila Bay

On the evening of April 30, 1898, Commodore George Dewey sailed his squadron of six ships into Manila Bay. Early the next morning, he moved through Manila Bay and within six hours destroyed the entire Spanish fleet. Spanish shore **batteries** and ships caused little damage to the American ships. The U.S. Navy now controlled the waters around the Philippines.

February 25, 1898.

Dewey, Hong Kong.

~~Secret and Confidential~~

    Order the Squadron except Monocacy to Hong Kong. Keep full of coal. In the event of declaration war Spain, your duty will be to see that the Spanish squadron does not leave the Asiatic coast and then offensive operations in Philipine Islands. Keep Olympia until further orders.

Roosevelt

Admiral William Thomas Sampson (1840–1902)

Before the War

William Thomas Sampson was born in the state of New York on February 9, 1840. He attended college at the **U.S. Naval Academy,** graduating first in his class in 1861. In 1862, Sampson served in the **Civil War** for the U.S. Navy.

During the War

Admiral Sampson commanded the U.S. Navy **fleet** in the Atlantic Ocean, sending ships to **blockade** Santiago Harbor. The entire Spanish fleet was trapped in the harbor and destroyed as they tried to leave.

After the War

William Sampson made the Navy his life-long career. In 1899, he took command of the Boston Navy Yard until he retired in 1902. Three months after his retirement, Admiral Sampson died. He is buried in **Arlington National Cemetery** near Washington, D.C.

In 1886, William Sampson returned to the U.S. Naval Academy to be the **superintendent.**

1898 Gazette

The Sinking of the USS *Maine*

Before war on Spain was declared, the United States anchored a Navy battleship, the USS *Maine*, in Havana Harbor to help calm fears about the safety of American citizens in Cuba. Soon after it arrived, the *Maine* exploded and sank. Some blamed the Spanish; some thought it was an accident. In 1898, William Sampson was part of a team of Navy investigators to report that a mine caused the explosion. The Spanish government denied being involved, and even today, no one can agree on a definite cause.

The Spanish Army

The Spanish Army was not well prepared to defend their colonies of Cuba, Puerto Rico, and the Philippines. Being a great distance from Spain, it was difficult to resupply their soldiers.

Uniforms

The basic uniform for the Spanish soldier was a shirt and pair of pants made of a white cotton material with thin, blue stripes. They were given straw hats with a black band. Officers wore a gold or silver metal piece in their hat to show that they were officers. Otherwise, they wore the same uniform as the men they commanded.

Even though the basic uniform was similar for all soldiers of the Spanish Army, different colored trims indicated the specific branches. Soldiers were issued shoes and boots, but it was not unusual to see rope-soled sandals on some.

1898 Gazette

Colors of the different branches of service were:

- **Infantry**—green
- **Cavalry**—red
- **Artillery**—blue

Some of the equipment issued to a Spanish Army soldier was:

- a blanket;
- a raincoat;
- a haversack—to carry small articles, including mess equipment (a spoon, a knife, a fork, a tin cup, and a container that was used as a dish);
- a rifle—the basic weapon of the army; and
- a cartridge belt—to carry bullets for the rifle.

23

Though the Spanish troops were outnumbered, their determination, ability, and bravery often delayed the advance of U.S. troops.

Strategy

Spanish Army soldiers were familiar with the geography and more used to the climate of these islands than were the American soldiers. They used the hills and heavy jungle growth on the islands to their advantage. They dug **trenches** on the hillsides, piling dirt in front for protection. In addition to the natural protection from plant growth, they placed obstacles and barbed wire in front of the mounds to disrupt the attacking army. The soldiers hid in the trenches and fired their rifles upon the oncoming army.

Although the Spanish Army was more familiar with the countryside, the Americans outnumbered them. It was only a matter of time before they were defeated.

The Spanish Navy

Dangers of Wooden Ships

After the United States declared war on Spain, Spanish naval leaders realized that their **fleet** of mostly older, wooden-**hulled** ships was no match for the more modern, steel-hulled ships of the U.S. Navy. Wooden ships presented a great danger in battle. Exploding shells caused wooden ships to catch fire and caused the wood to shatter, sending sharp pieces flying in all directions.

1898 Gazette

Admiral Cervera's best ship had to quickly sail from Spain to the Caribbean Sea without all of its guns installed to meet the American fleet.

Preparedness of the Spanish Fleet

The Spanish Navy was not prepared for war. The Spanish government did not have the money to maintain their ships, provide supplies, and properly train sailors. Because of this lack of supplies, training, and poor condition of the ships, **morale** was low among Spanish sailors.

Without a strong Navy, Spanish armies defending Spain's island **colonies** could not receive necessary equipment and supplies to fight a war, and therefore they could not succeed.

Spanish naval officers and sailors gather on the Reina Cristina *before it was destroyed in the Battle of Manila Bay.*

The Emperador Carlos V *(left) was one of only a few steel-hulled, modern warships of the Spanish Navy. It was also one of the few Spanish ships to escape destruction during the war.*

Admiral Patricio Montojo y Pasarón (1839–1917)

Before the War
Patricio Montojo y Pasarón was born in Spain on September 7, 1839. In 1852, he became a naval **cadet** at a Spanish military academy. Upon completing his education, Montojo began his career in the Spanish Navy, fighting in the Philippine Islands and then commanding ships in Cuba.

During the War
In 1898, Montojo commanded the Spanish Squadron that was destroyed at the Battle of Manila Bay in the Philippines.

After the War
Admiral Montojo was ordered to return to Spain to explain the defeat at Manila Bay. The Spanish Navy found him guilty of not performing his duties properly. This decision was later reversed, but Montojo was dismissed from the navy. Montojo died in Madrid, Spain, on September 30, 1917.

1898 Gazette
Montojo's sons, Eugenio and Patricio, also took part in the Battle of Manila Bay. Both Admiral Montojo and Eugenio were wounded in action.

Montojo was the commander-in-chief of the Spanish Navy in the Philippines during the Spanish-American War.

Admiral Pascual Cervera y Topete (1839–1909)

Before the War
Pascual Cervera was born in Spain on February 18, 1839. After completing his education at the Naval Academy of San Fernando in Spain, Cervera began a life-long career in the Spanish Navy.

During the War
In 1898, Admiral Cervera commanded a **fleet** of ships sent to protect Spain's **colonies** in the Caribbean Sea from the United States. After he sailed his ships into Santiago Bay, Cuba, the U.S. fleet **blockaded** it. His ships tried to escape the blockade, but were unsuccessful. All the Spanish ships were destroyed, and Cervera was captured. After two months he was released and returned to Spain.

After the War
Cervera continued to work for the Spanish government until his retirement in 1907. He returned to southern Spain where he died in 1909.

Pascual Cervera had a long naval career, from the time he entered the Naval College in Spain at age 13 until his retirement at age 68.

1898 Gazette

Cervera wrote a letter to his cousin, Juan Spottorno, before the start of the war. He believed that the war would be a mistake:

Dear Juan. It seems that the conflict (war) with the United States is being reconsidered... and every day I am more and more confident... that it would be a great national calamity...

Conclusion

Soldiers and sailors from the countries of Spain, the United States, Cuba, Puerto Rico, and the Philippines fought in the Spanish-American War. Some fought for independence, some fought to defend a **colony,** and others fought for human rights. The countries they fought for either gained independence, lost their claim to land, or gained new lands for their nation. All soldiers and sailors fought bravely for their cause.

As a Result of the War: Spain

Spain lost more than 50,000 men and their major colonies of Cuba, Puerto Rico, and the Philippine Islands. They would need to rebuild their military defenses to regain respect in the world as a strong nation.

Spanish troops wait to ship out at Santiago Harbor, Cuba, after Spain's loss at the Battle of San Juan Heights.

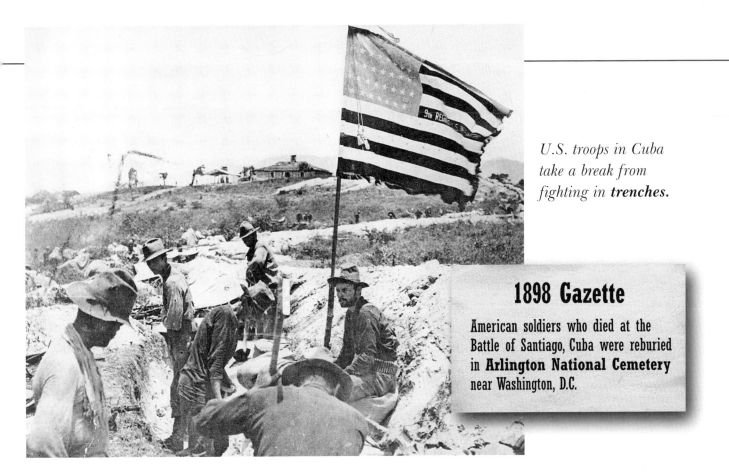

*U.S. troops in Cuba take a break from fighting in **trenches**.*

1898 Gazette

American soldiers who died at the Battle of Santiago, Cuba were reburied in **Arlington National Cemetery** near Washington, D.C.

As a Result of the War: the United States

The United States emerged from the war as a world power. They now needed to strengthen their military defense system to stay a world power. The U.S. gained naval bases in Cuba and the Pacific. Army schools were created, officers were chosen to make military plans and policies for future situations, special groups such as a medical and army nurse corps were organized, and the **National Guard** was strengthened.

Even though the Spanish-American War was short, the U.S. victory would not have been possible without the thousands of volunteers.

…When the squadrons meet, when it's **fleet** to fleet
And **front** to front with Spain,
…When the guns shall flash and the shot shall crash…
When the rattling blasts from the armored masts
Are hurling their deadliest rain,…
Remember, remember the Maine!

from *Battle Song* by Robert Burns Wilson

The United States declared war on Spain on April 25, 1898. The peace treaty to end the war was signed on December 10, 1898.

Glossary

Arlington National Cemetery   place in Arlington, Virginia, where casualties from wars in which the U.S. fought are buried

artillery   cannons

assassinate   to murder a government leader, usually for political reasons

Asiatic Squadron   group of U.S. Navy ships that patrolled the Pacific Ocean

battery   artillery unit of men, cannons, equipment, and horses

blockade   to position ships to prevent supplies or other ships from entering a port

cadet   student in training to become an officer in the army, navy, or air force

cavalry   soldiers who rode horses

Civil War   war fought in the United States from 1861 to 1865 between the Union (North) and Confederate (South) states over issues of slavery and states' rights

colony   territory settled by people from other countries who still had loyalty to those other countries

Congress   men who represented the individual states in the U.S. government, either in the House of Representatives or the Senate

enlist   to volunteer for military service

fleet   group of ships

force   group of soldiers

fortification   structure built to protect soldiers from an attacking enemy

front   place where fighting is happening between enemy forces

frontier   part of a settled area that lies next to a region that is still wild

hull   sides and bottom of a boat or ship

infantry   foot soldiers

khaki   strong, yellow-brown cloth usually used to make military uniforms

Medal of Honor   highest military decoration given to members of the U.S. armed forces for bravery in combat

morale   state of mind of a person or group working toward a goal

National Guard   unit of soldiers for a particular state

oath   statement in which a person agrees to keep a promise

politics   government affairs

regiment   group of soldiers

regular army   group of full-time soldiers

resign   to give up a job, membership, or other position in a group

resistance fighter   person who fights or works against someone or something

running mate   person who takes part in a contest or election along with someone else

segregate   to set apart from others, usually racial groups

slouch hat   soft, felt hat with a wide brim

superintendent   person in charge of a school system or some other type of large organization

transport   to move from one place to another

trench   long, deep ditch used by the military for shelter from gunfire and to strengthen defensive positions

U.S. Naval Academy   school were students go to become officers in the navy

Further Reading

Collins, Mary. *The Spanish-American War.* Danbury, Conn.: Children's Press, 1998.

McNeese, Tim. *Remember the Maine!: The Spanish-American War Begins.* Greensboro, N.C.: Morgan Reynolds, Inc., 2001.

Wukovitz, John F. *The Spanish-American War.* Farmington Hills, Mich.: Gale Group, 2001.

Historical Places to Visit

Arlington National Cemetery
Administrative Building
Arlington, Virginia 22211
Visitor information: (703) 695-3250
The mainmast of the USS *Maine*, which was salvaged and brought to the cemetery, marks the graves of 62 known and 167 unknown crewmen lost in the explosion of this ship—an event that sparked public demand to declare war on Spain in 1898. Two other monuments honor Spanish-American War nurses and the "Rough Riders."

The Navy Museum
Washington Navy Yard
Building 76
805 Kidder Breese SE
Washington, D.C. 20374-5060
Visitor information: (202) 433-4882
This museum, which presents an overview of the history of the U.S. Navy, includes exhibits on the U.S. Navy's activities during the Spanish-American War.

Henry B. Plant Museum (Hotel Tampa Bay)
401 W. Kennedy Blvd.
Tampa, Florida 33606-1450
Visitor information: (813) 254-1891
Visit exhibits about how Henry Plant and the Tampa Bay Hotel played a role in the Spanish-American War as the embarkation headquarters of the U.S. Army.

U.S. Naval Academy, Armel-Leftwich Visitor Center
52 King George Street (Gate 1)
Annapolis, Maryland 21402
Visitor information: (410) 263-6933
The United States Naval Academy was established in 1845 to prepare young men and women to become professional officers in the U.S. Navy and Marine Corps. The visitor center features interactive exhibits, pictorial displays, and guided tours on the history and traditions of the Naval Academy.

Index